COULD IT HAPPEN HERE?

About the Authors

ANDREW BLICK is professor of politics and contemporary history in the department of political economy, King's College London, where he co-directs the Centre for British Democracy. He is the author of books including *Electrified Democracy: The Internet and the United Kingdom Parliament in History* and *Beyond Magna Carta: A Constitution for the United Kingdom*. Before entering academia, he worked in the UK Parliament and at Number 10 Downing Street. His PhD on the history of special advisers in UK government was supervised by Peter Hennessy. He is director of the Constitution Society, an educational charity for the promotion of knowledge of constitutional issues.

PETER HENNESSY is Attlee professor of contemporary British history at Queen Mary University of London. He is the author of several books including a postwar trilogy (*Never Again: Britain 1945–51*; *Having It So Good: Britain in the Fifties*; *Winds of Change: Britain in the Early Sixties*). His most recent work is *On the Back of an Envelope: A Life in Writing*. He is a fellow of the British Academy and an honorary fellow of St John's College, Cambridge. He sits in the House of Lords as an independent crossbench peer.

Haus Curiosities

Inspired by the topical pamphlets of the interwar years, as well as by Einstein's advice to 'never lose a holy curiosity', the series presents short works of opinion and analysis by notable figures. Under the guidance of the series editor, Peter Hennessy, Haus Curiosities have been published since 2014. Welcoming contributions from a diverse pool of authors, the series aims to reinstate the concise and incisive booklet as a powerful strand of politico-literary life, amplifying the voices of those who have something urgent to say about a topical theme.

The Constitution Society

The Constitution Society is an independent educational foundation. It works to promote public understanding of the UK constitution and to encourage informed debate between legislators, academics, and the public about proposals for constitutional change. The Society is a registered, entirely independent charity with no connection to any political party. For funding, the Society relies on individual donations and grants from educational trusts and foundations. You can learn more about the work of the Constitution Society at www.consoc.org.uk.

HAUS CURIOSITIES

COULD IT HAPPEN HERE?
The Day a Prime Minister Refuses to Resign

Peter Hennessy and Andrew Blick

THE CONSTITUTION SOCIETY

First published by Haus Publishing in 2025
4 Cinnamon Row
London SW11 3TW
www.hauspublishing.com

A CIP catalogue record for this book is
available from the British Library

ISBN: 978-1-914979-18-7
eISBN: 978-1-914979-19-4

Typeset in Garamond by MacGuru Ltd

Printed in Czechia

Contents

In memory of Giles Radice,
friend and mentor

A Profound Constitutional Breakdown

*We don't have a written constitution, we
have constitutional arrangements ...*
Lord Lisvane, former clerk of the House of Commons
(16 July 2024, day of the State Opening of Parliament)

*If liberal democracy fails in the 21st century, as it failed
in the twentieth, to construct a humane, prosperous,
and peaceful world, it will invite the rise of alternative
creeds apt to be based, like fascism and communism,
on flight from freedom and surrender to authority.*
Arthur Schlesinger Jr. ('Has Democracy a Future?', 1997)

The 'voice of sanity' is getting hoarse ...
Seamus Heaney ('Whatever You Say, Say Nothing', 1975)

We have no wish to cause alarm. We are not devotees of
the 'what if?' school of history. We can scarcely believe
we are trailing these thoughts and possibilities in the
pages to come. Until the summer of 2024, it simply
would not have occurred to us to do so. But, with the
significant surge of the hard Right in Western Europe,

more than a flicker of it in the British election debate of June to July 2024, plus the still vivid memory of how easy it proved for some of the conventions and decencies of political behaviour to be swept aside during the Johnson years in No. 10 (which we discussed in an earlier treatment, *The Bonfire of the Decencies*), there lurks in the British political air a tang of unease.

As we began to write, a wave of deeply worrying disturbances disfigured a range of big cities and large towns after far-Right demonstrators, feeding off disinformation and lies about the murderer of three young girls at a dance school in Southport, sought to foment what some of them plainly wished would follow – a 'race war'. The still very new Prime Minister sought, through a mixture of countermeasures and deterrence, to blunt the violence and unleash the law upon the perpetrators.

The King, carefully judging the timing, content, and its means of communication, waited until the end of the week of disturbances before making his intervention. On Friday 10 August, his Buckingham Palace spokesman let it be known that the King had talked on the phone to the Prime Minister and senior police figures, telling them he had been 'greatly encouraged' by the way they had countered the 'aggression and criminality from a few with the compassion and resilience of the many' describing his 'heartfelt thanks' to the police and the emergency services. He had been greatly encouraged, too, 'by the many examples of community spirit' that the disturbances had brought forth. Underscoring one of the major themes of Charles III's reign, the Palace spokesman said: 'It remains his Majesty's hope that shared values of mutual respect and understanding will continue to strengthen and unite the nation.'

Though in no way wishing to suggest a level of peril is close that might eventually inject the blight of authoritarianism into mainstream British politics, the experiences of July to August 2024 did add to a sense that we could be edging towards a coarse, deeply undesirable, and occasionally violence-tinged system of politics that itself could bring about an authoritarian administration in the Cabinet Room at some point in the next fifteen to twenty years.

As a consequence of these factors, a political and constitutional contingency that scarcely dare speak its name is this: if, through a series of mischances, we were to find ourselves with an authoritarian government that refused to budge after the country, in a general election, had voted against them or produced a hung result leading to a deal between rival parties in order to command a majority in the House of Commons. How might they be removed and prevented from abusing their position while they retained office? We explore this particular scenario as a possibility in itself, but in doing so also provide a basis for considering a wider range of potential outcomes that could come about in the context of a rise of authoritarian politics, and its intersection with the UK constitution.

Part One, The Limpet Prime Minister, is an account of the projected circumstance which is the basis for this book, placing it in the context of the UK democratic system.

Part Two, Protecting the System, considers the existing instruments (written and unwritten) available to those wishing to deter or counter this scenario and to restrict the potential for malpractice on the part of the recalcitrant premier pending their being ousted. It also discusses the human defences – that is, the office holders who might come into play. It is not only their offices that count, but that they, as individuals, 'do the right thing', as one insider put it; 'the more they act in concert, the likelier you are to prise off the limpet'. Finally, Part Two sketches out means by which we might construct stronger and better-understood defences of the British way of parliamentary democracy than exist at present.

Part Three, The Ten-Year Stress Test, sets out key constitutional developments since the 2014 referendum on Scottish independence, as a kind of ready reckoner of what happened next. It also partly carries a cumulative explanation of the stress experienced by the mysterious entity we call our 'unwritten constitution'.

As for the authors, we fervently hope that what follows is the most redundant piece of work either of us has ever published. We would be truly happy if, in the years to come, a young PhD student found our words in an obscure corner of a second-hand bookshop and thoroughly derided us for wasting their time and that of any reader we might have diverted from other things.

Peter Hennessy and Andrew Blick, November 2024

Part One

The Limpet Prime Minister: A System Under Threat[1]

> *Freedom justifies government. The*
> *forms of freedom show us how.*
> Professor Timothy Snyder (*On Freedom*, 2024)

Imagine a scenario: a hard-Right government loses its majority at a general election that produces a 'hung' Parliament. This could also apply to an extremist administration from the hard Left of the political spectrum, but for present purposes our scenario is drawn from the hard Right.

Its leader chooses to follow the 1923–4 precedent by deciding to meet Parliament with a King's Speech, which it loses in a House of Commons vote as the other parties coalesce against it – indicating the likelihood that a coalition agreement or a confidence-and-supply arrangement could command the confidence of the House of Commons.*

---

* At the December 1923 General Election, the governing Conservative Party under Stanley Baldwin, while remaining

The hard-Right Prime Minister, however, refuses to budge. They say they will not resign as theirs is still the largest single party in the Commons, and that a stitch-up by their rivals would represent a denial of the will of the people: one which they might, if thwarted, demonstrate by taking to the streets.

Against a mounting backdrop of crisis at home, an increasingly frenzied media of all kinds, and turbulence for the pound sterling in the global money markets, the House of Commons finds itself in truly uncharted territory. The Speaker refuses to take the Chair. They order the Clerks not to sit at the Table. The Mace is not carried into the Chamber. The Chaplain refuses to pray. The House of Commons cannot function without this combination of ritual, worship, and choreography. The Speaker announces that they are going to see the King, to inquire directly what his intentions are.

Over the course of three speeches, delivered during his first few days as sovereign, King Charles III issued the following declarations (this is history rather than scenario):

In that [Anglican] faith and the values it inspires, I have been brought up to cherish a sense of duty to

---

the largest in the House of Commons, lost its overall majority. Labour and the Liberals between them could command a majority. Baldwin chose to face the Commons in January 2024, and having lost a confidence vote, resigned. He was succeeded as premier by the Labour leader Ramsay MacDonald, who the Liberals under Herbert Asquith had opted to provide with parliamentary support.

others, and to hold in the greatest respect the precious traditions, freedoms and responsibilities of our unique history and our system of parliamentary government. As the Queen herself did with such unswerving devotion, I too now solemnly pledge myself, throughout the remaining time God grants me, to uphold the constitutional principles at the heart of our nation.

Address to the nation and Commonwealth
(9 September 2022)[2]

I am deeply aware of this great inheritance and of the duties and heavy responsibilities of Sovereignty which have now passed to me. In taking up these responsibilities, I shall strive to follow the inspiring example I have been set in upholding constitutional government ...

Declaration (10 September 2022)[3]

... the precious principles of constitutional government which lie at the heart of our nation ...

Reply to addresses of condolence at Westminster Hall
(12 September 2022)[4]

King Charles is quite plainly a man highly sensitive not just to the niceties and parameters of British constitutional monarchy, but also to the whole mesh of requirements that need to be kept in good repair if the *wider* constitution is to continue to provide the sensitivity, continuity, and resilience that it has in the past.

The operational norm that the Palace applies if a general election produces a hung result is this: the political parties sort out among themselves who or what combination of MPs can command a majority, or a working arrangement based on so-called 'confidence and supply', before the incumbent prime minister advises the monarch who to send for as their next prime minister. In Palace shorthand, 'we want the cameras to be concentrated at the Whitehall end of The Mall, not ours'. In other words, as Ken Stowe, principal private secretary to three prime ministers, put it to one of us (PH) in 1997: 'It's all about good chaps. 'Fraid so.' It was so – and it still is. Buckingham Palace is a thoroughly 'good chaps' operation.*

But, in our 'limpet' scenario, the 'good chaps' theory might fracture into so much constitutional wreckage. What would the King be facing when the Speaker came to call? We doubt that he would rush into action. He and his private secretary can consult whoever they wish to gauge opinion and flesh out possibilities and would, no doubt, do so with immense care.

Would the King, as a first step, summon the limpet

---

* When referring to 'good chaps', we do not seek to convey unquestioning approval of traditional methods of constitutional management. We also recognise that the term reflects the social hierarchies of the era which produced it. However, it remains relevant given that no clear replacement for the 'good chaps' approach has been found and the term is widely employed inside and outside governing circles to describe the self-regulation on which we rely.

and *encourage* him to do the decent thing and resign? He would surely *advise* him to follow that course of action and *warn* him of the constitutional and behavioural consequences for the realm if he did not (Walter Bagehot, famously, said the monarch had the rights to encourage, advise, and warn).

If the limpet returned to No. 10 unpersuaded by the King and still set on his constitution-wrecking mission, the monarch could summon each of the other party leaders in turn to assess the likelihood of their combining to form a government.

At this point, against a background of anxiety and maybe even disturbances across the land at home and turbulence in the money markets abroad, would the Palace announce that the King would be broadcasting to his people that evening?

It would be presumptuous of us to suggest his thoughts and the vocabulary he might deploy, but we would be very surprised if 'the precious principles of constitutional government' were not in there somewhere.

The big immediate question? Whether the King would announce that he was reaching for his personal prerogative of dissolving Parliament and thereby triggering another general election (only the monarch can do this; just as only a monarch can appoint a prime minister).

The squatter Prime Minister would no doubt portray this as:

The King versus The People.

We are convinced that the vast bulk of 'The People' would not see it like that. They – and the Crown services in uniform or civvies – would rally around their monarch.

It may seem a tad perverse to be floating such a scenario in the months following a general election which gave a Keir Starmer-led, thoroughly social-democratic government a majority of 174 seats in the House of Commons. We cannot conceive of a former director of public prosecutions turned prime minister behaving in such a way. But it is precisely when there *is* no immediate danger that the circumstances attending possible future constitutional crises can be aired for considered debate, without the danger of the authors being misrepresented. And we do not believe that such a crisis in ten or twenty years' time is unthinkable. In media interviews over the weekend of 20 to 21 July 2024, barely three weeks after Starmer's triumph and before the rash of street disturbances, three of his senior ministers – Rachel Reeves, chancellor of the Exchequer; Wes Streeting, health secretary; and David Lammy, foreign secretary – raised the risk of a rise of British authoritarianism.[5] The public share such concerns. Polling conducted in August 2024, after the summer riots, showed that 74 per cent of people in Great Britain were concerned about rising religious extremism; 73 per cent about increasing right-wing extremism; and 70 per cent about the condition of democracy in Britain.[6] In October 2024, the director-general of the Security Service, Ken McCallum, provided a public update on threats. In discussing the countering of terrorist threats, he explained that 25 per cent of the work of his agency involved right-wing extremist terrorism (and 75 per cent Islamist terrorism). Threats also came in the form of interference from foreign states, in particular China, Iran, and Russia.[7]

The components of democracy

Liberal democracies have much to lose. They are the accumulation of centuries of wisdom, experience, and careful institution-building, and represent the flowering of particular states of mind. But their decay – possibly their destruction – could be the work of a decade or two, perhaps less, even in those countries whose values seem most securely rooted in the rich soils that nurture them.

On Monday 29 January 2024, the House of Lords gave a second reading to the Sunak government's Rwanda (Safety) Bill (now an Act). One of us (PH) delivered a short, anxious speech in the mid-afternoon, expressing his fears for the rule of law if the legislation were to pass through all its parliamentary stages and receive the royal assent in a few weeks' time (it was being rushed through as part of an emergency procedure).

Gary Gibbon, political editor of *Channel 4 News* sent an email saying he would be using a clip in his piece that evening and wondering just how embedded liberal democracy really is in 2020s Britain.

This was the extract Gary used:

In the few minutes it takes [the Rwanda (Safety) Act 2024] to pass down The Mall and across the tip of St. James's Park on its return journey to Whitehall, our country will change. For the Government will have removed us from the list of 'rule of law' nations. We shall be living in a different land; breathing a different air in a significantly diminished Kingdom. My Lords, is that what any of us *really* want?[8]

Gary, in a subsequent conversation, wondered about that last sentence, particularly in the context of a recent piece of opinion surveying among the 18–35-year-old age group which indicated that, globally, 42 per cent supported military rule, as opposed to 20 per cent of those older than them.[9]

PH discussed Gary's thoughts with another media friend – Gordon Corera, the former BBC security correspondent – having recently had with him a conversation about the condition of the UK, which included the wider theme of the health of British liberal democracy. We concluded it might be a good start if we wrote down the ingredients of that liberal democracy as currently practised within our shores.

Long-settled political societies generally don't feel the need to do this. If you live here, you just know. It's all part of the mix of mental muscle memories, 'tacit understandings', common instincts, shared aversions, and organic adaptations that together mulch into the topsoil of the national allotment off which we feed – more *Gardeners' Question Time* than written constitution.

Notions of 'national character' are, quite rightly, treated with a high degree of suspicion by historians. But the idea of a national 'political consciousness' – what Roy Jenkins called the 'national mind'[10] – may offer a promising, if imprecise, concept which helps capture the ebb and flow of widely shared values and expectations about how our nation should conduct its collective life and civic behaviour.

In his classic study of 'The Structure of Human History', *Plough, Sword and Book*, Ernest Gellner, the fabled social anthropologist, wrote:

> One crucial aspect of the way in which human societies maintain and transmit their distinctive features can be called *culture*. Culture can be defined as the set of concepts and terms of which a given population acts and thinks ... culture consists of sets of acquired characteristics ... a distinct way of doing things which characterises a given community ...[11]

The constitutional slice of a nation's culture is critical to the maintenance and transmission of core values, which is why Britain's lack of a written document makes the task of transmission from one generation to the next so taxing and crucial. Drafting a set of ingredients for the version of liberal democracy that we deploy on our islands feels distinctly un-British and odd. But here follows our attempt to capture the components of a liberal (UK) democracy:

The 'inner core' of indispensables
- Regular free elections to a sovereign legislature, with public trust in the validity of the outcomes at this and other levels – such as in devolved polities or in referendums
- A non-political head of state in the form of a constitutional monarch
- The rule of law
- An independent judiciary recruited through a non-politicised appointments process
- Mutual respect between Westminster and devolved polities
- A firm desire on the part of all the main players in the constitutional system to uphold the key rules and conventions underpinning it, whether they are tacit or explicit
- An overall aversion to political violence, a lack of access to weapons – especially automatic weapons and ammunition – and a general dislike of the idea of civilian gun ownership

Enablers (institutional)
- A non-politicised Civil Service whose senior ranks are not replaced following a change of government

- Political parties that pursue their competition for power with an acceptance, without caveat, of electoral outcomes and confidence votes in the House of Commons
- Recognition by ministers that they are accountable to Parliament and that they need to cooperate with its work in good faith
- A free press/media, coupled with a high degree of trust in a considerable proportion of public information sources, particularly the reliability of the BBC. If this confidence is lacking, then more dubious providers, such as those found via social media, can fill the vacuum, to the detriment of meaningful, considered discourse

Human rights
- Continuing incorporation in UK law of a core set of human rights, as set out in texts including the European Convention on Human Rights, a treaty that first came into force in 1953 and in the drafting of which the UK had a crucial input. Among the rights protected by the Convention are the right to life; the prohibition of torture; the right to privacy and family life; freedom of expression, assembly, and association; the right to a fair trial; freedom of belief; and the prohibition of discrimination. In general, accompanying these legally protected rights, a strong culture of social tolerance is essential

Enablers (material)
- A 'mixed' economy with an energetic private sector that is sufficiently productive and incentivised to finance a high level of health, education, and welfare, generating sufficient resources to ease the employment/human transitions required to harvest the fruits of scientific and technological advance

Intangibles
- Sustenance of a society with the possibility of substantial peaceful change/regeneration without disturbance or violence
- Maintaining the flow of benefits from free 'penumbral' institutions, such as universities, research institutes, learned societies, and professional bodies
- A high level of public trust in expertise and knowledge
- An honours system that enhances the above and recognises true merit, public service, voluntary service, and bravery
- A presumption of decency as social superglue and a deep aversion to threats against individuals

Protectors
- A well-trained, disciplined, and publicly trusted police force
- A cadre of highly trained, disciplined, and publicly trusted armed forces

- An intelligence community, with strong overseas liaisons, subject to ministerial and parliamentary oversight
- A set of alliances (NATO pre-eminently) that act as force-multipliers and collective defence for the UK
- Membership of multilateral international institutions plus adherence to the international laws and conventions that go with them and increase the chance of dispute resolution without resorting to physical conflict

That, by any standards, is a cluster of practices, procedures, aspirations, and relationships worth defending with the last ounce of strength and intelligence we possess as a country and a people. Those contents, taken together, also provide a set of norms and tests against which we can judge our performance as an open society and a rule-of-law nation. But what are the main rules – both hard and soft in nature – that might protect these values if they came under threat from a limpet prime minister?

Part Two

Protecting the System

We ask our readers to imagine the Speaker's car nearing the end of The Mall as he travels west for his emergency audience with the King, as the national and world media descends on London SW1.

If the Speaker had asked us for an audit of the defences – human, structural, and constitutional, written and unwritten – British parliamentary democracy has at its disposal, this is, as far as we can discern its nooks, crannies, intricacies, and mysteries, what it would look like.

Legislation and conventions

We start with the Security Service Act 1989, as it is the only statute which describes 'parliamentary democracy' directly as part of the defence of the realm and the personal duties of the director-general of the Security Service (MI5). This reference is included in Section 1 of the Act as follows:

1 The Security Service.
(1) There shall continue to be a Security Service

(in this Act referred to as 'the Service') under the authority of the Secretary of State.

(2) The function of the Service shall be the protection of national security and, in particular, its protection against threats from espionage, terrorism and sabotage, from the activities of agents of foreign powers and from actions intended to overthrow or undermine parliamentary democracy by political, industrial or violent means.

Section 2 of the 1989 Act describes the office of director-general and gives them a clear role in preventing the Security Service from participating in democratically inappropriate activities. It reads (as amended):

2 The Director-General.

(1) The operations of the Service shall continue to be under the control of a Director-General appointed by the Secretary of State.

(2) The Director-General shall be responsible for the efficiency of the Service and it shall be his duty to ensure—

   (a) that there are arrangements for securing that no information is obtained by the Service except so far as necessary for the proper discharge of its functions or disclosed by it except so far as necessary for that purpose or for the purpose of the prevention or detection of serious crime or for the purpose of any criminal proceedings; and

(b) that the Service does not take any action to
further the interests of any political party ...
(4) The Director-General shall make an annual
report on the work of the Service to the Prime
Minister and the Secretary of State and may at any
time report to either of them on any matter relating
to its work.

These provisions are designed to protect the Security
Service from misuse for partisan ends. (The Intelligence
Services Act 1994 also contains provisions that prevent
the two other main agencies, GCHQ and SIS, from
taking action that furthers the interests of a political
party.) It differs from the other agencies in that they
receive their tasks directly from the government, while
the director-general of the Security Service decides the
work it will carry out. In a limpet scenario, these insu-
lations could become significant. The director-general
might, for instance, be able to launch an investigation
into whether a foreign power had links to the prime minister and their project. To do so, however, might test the
so-called 'Wilson Doctrine', established by the Labour
Prime Minister Harold Wilson in 1966 and placed on
a statutory basis by the Investigatory Powers Act 2016
(Section 26). The rule is that the interception of the
communications of MPs (and of members of devolved
legislatures) can only take place with the approval of the
prime minister.

Other laws have created specific powers intended

to address movements committed to undermining the democratic system, and as such there is a great pile of counterterrorism legislation.[1] A recent act concerned with national security, however, is relevant, as it deals with the specific problem being addressed here: that there may be detectable in the activities of our authoritarian political movement the rattle of foreign coin. This threat has been already identified by the Parliamentary Intelligence and Security Committee, and who knows what technical feats will be possible by the 2030s.

In the context of concerns about foreign interference in political processes, the UK government introduced legislation that became the National Security Act 2023. It sought to prohibit coercion and misrepresentation (Section 15) directed towards interference with (Section 14) the exercise of human rights, the performance of public functions, and participation in political and legal processes; or towards compromising the interests or the safety of the UK. The Act sought to protect the integrity of all tiers of governance, from local to UK level, and of elections and referendums.

Other legislation deals with the possibility of serious public disruption or emergency, whether civil or military in nature. The UK has a history of expansive provision in this field. For instance, a wide range of measures were created and implemented during the Second World War, including substantial detentions without trial of people believed to pose a security risk.[2] During the Cold War period, there were plans in place that would be implemented during the transition to war period to provide for regional, non-parliamentary, emergency rule in the event of conflict, drawn up in the wake of the Cuban missile crisis. A draft statute, the Emergency Powers Defence Bill, was ready and printed.[3]

The contemporary successor to such provisions is the Civil Contingencies Act 2004. Part 2 of this law allows ministers to introduce emergency legislation in defined circumstances. Potentially, it could be employed by our hypothetical authoritarian leader, or for the purposes of dealing with civil unrest in the aftermath of their removal.[4] Its definition of an emergency includes (Section 19): 'an event or situation which threatens serious damage to human welfare in the United Kingdom or in a Part or region'; and 'war, or terrorism, which threatens serious damage to the security of the United Kingdom.' The threat to human welfare can include possible or actual 'loss of human life ... human illness or injury ... damage to property ... disruption of a supply of money, food, water, energy or fuel ... disruption of a system of communication ... disruption of facilities for transport'. Any regulations issued under the Act lapse after seven days if not approved by both Houses of Parliament (Section 27). The regulations can accomplish changes the same as those that could be achieved by an Act of Parliament, but are subject to some limitations: for instance, they cannot be used to alter protected parts of the 2004 Act itself or the Human Rights Act 1998.

The Covid-19 pandemic was an incident of the type

which Part 2 of the 2004 Act was intended to provide for a response to. In the event, however, fresh legislation – the Coronavirus Act 2020 – was passed, rather than relying upon the 2004 Act. Yet even this new legislation was not much deployed, with the government preferring to utilise earlier public-health legislation – the Public Health (Control of Disease) Act 1984 – for the imposition of extensive lockdown measures.

All of the measures discussed so far, except perhaps those alluded to in the Security Service Act 1989, are aimed at dealing with threats to the system from outside – either beyond the institutions of governance, or outside the country, or both, or perhaps passing unseen and border-blind through the air. They assume people of good faith (once known as 'good chaps') hold positions of responsibility. They were certainly not designed with the possibility in mind that people at the very top might themselves be the problem. Indeed, in such an unfortunate scenario, some of these instruments could be deployed by such individuals for malign purposes. At points in the past, observers of UK politics have examined the possibility of groups hostile to democracy coming to power through the system itself. In 1978, for instance, the Conservative politician and future cabinet minister under Margaret Thatcher and John Major, William Waldegrave, warned that:

> our constitution is dangerously vulnerable to capture
> by the minority who can get hold of a political party

which then, for one reason or another, gains a majority in the House. This state of affairs make [sic] it all too plausible that the worst nightmare of Conservative or Liberal alike – the capture of the executive by a totalitarian clique which would subsequently impose its intellectually disreputable uncertainties at the barrel of a gun – could become a reality.[5]

While the scenario we explore in this work involves a prime minister of the hard Right, Waldegrave was focused more on threats from the Left (though there were also grounds for concern about the Right at the time[6]), but the concerns he raised were similar to those we address in the current work. Yet, despite the somewhat recurring nature of such apprehensions, we have found no evidence to suggest that there has ever been serious planning for such a contingency by the official agencies or departments concerned.

There is, however, a long-established legislative constitutional safety mechanism that could be relevant. The Parliament Acts 1911 and 1949 make it possible, when the House of Commons and House of Lords disagree over the contents of a bill, for the Commons ultimately to override the Lords, and present a bill in its preferred form for royal assent. Governments, which normally have absolute majorities in the Commons, are therefore in a position, if determined to do so, to drive through legislation that is democratically inappropriate. The Lords can only delay most laws for a little over a year, over two parliamentary sessions. But an important exception to this rule, as set out in the 1911 Act (as amended in 1949), involves the length of Parliaments. A bill that seeks to extend them beyond five years (as happened during the First and Second World Wars), therefore also delaying the date of the next general election, remains subject to an absolute veto by the Lords. As the Act states:

> [Section] 2 Restriction of the powers of the House of Lords as to Bills rather than Money Bills
> If any Public Bill (other than a Money Bill or a Bill containing any provision to extend the maximum duration of Parliament beyond five years) is passed by the House of Commons in two successive sessions (whether of the same Parliament or not), and, having been sent up to the House of Lords at least one month before the end of the session, is rejected by the House of Lords in each of those sessions, that Bill shall, on its rejection for the second time by the House of Lords, unless the House of Commons direct to the contrary, be presented to His Majesty and become an Act of Parliament on the Royal Assent being signified thereto, notwithstanding that the House of Lords have not consented to the Bill ...

Alongside 'hard' law, also significant to our 'limpet' scenario is the 'soft' variety: a body of conventions, some existing in tacit form, some codified in documents such as the *Ministerial Code* and the *Cabinet Manual*.[7] It may, of course, be that by the time the scenario we envisage has come to pass, this kind of constitutional regulation will have been deliberately degraded by the political movement and leadership in question. A refusal on the part of a prime minister to leave office despite clearly losing the confidence of the House of Commons would amount to a direct assault on such established tenets. Nonetheless, those seeking to displace a mollusc premier from No. 10 Downing Street could refer to various understandings such as those contained in the *Cabinet Manual*, a text published in 2011 (now sorely in need of being updated) setting out, from the perspective of the UK executive, the core features of the UK system. The *Manual* states, for instance, that (paragraph 2.7):

> The ability of a government to command the confidence of the elected House of Commons is central to its authority to govern. It is tested by votes on motions of confidence, or no confidence.

Elsewhere in the text, the *Manual* states that (paragraph 2.12):

> Where an election does not result in an overall majority for a single party, the incumbent government remains in office unless and until the Prime Minister tenders his or her resignation and the Government's resignation to the Sovereign. An incumbent government is entitled to wait until the new Parliament has

met to see if it can command the confidence of the House of Commons, but is expected to resign if it becomes clear that it is unlikely to be able to command that confidence and there is a clear alternative.

These passages make it clear that the existence of any government rests in the consent of the Commons. At the same time, they also demonstrate that the maintenance of this principle rests more in good behaviour than hard power. In a hung-Parliament scenario, an administration that seems to have lost that confidence will resign because it is 'expected' to do so. If it chooses to ignore that expectation, problems begin.

The cast of players

Structures, systems, and rules are fundamentally important. But they all rely on having people within them who are committed to democratic values, and who are willing to assert themselves in fraught circumstances. They need buttressing and supporting. This would be one of the purposes of the Speaker's brief as he is escorted from his car by the King's Private Secretary and taken upstairs for his audience with the Monarch. We now deal in turn with the relevant office holders and consider what their function might be. A useful way of delineating the individuals and clusters of players is to see them as either the front or the back line in the defence of democracy. The politicians, crucially the speaker, are in the front line; the heads of the intelligence and security agencies, for example, would be the 'last resort' back line.

- The monarch, as head of state and commander-in-chief of the armed services
- The speaker of the House of Commons
- The prime minister and their Cabinet colleagues
- The leaders of the anti-authoritarian parties
- Parliament, including the House of Lords
- The chief of the defence staff
- The cabinet secretary
- The judiciary (first the High Court, then the Supreme Court)
- A handful of very senior officers in the secret services
- The permanent secretary to the Treasury (the supplier of government finances)
- The governor of the Bank of England (the government's lender of last resort)
- The comptroller and auditor general (ensurer that government spends money only in accordance with the wishes of Parliament)
- The clerk of the House of Commons

We will now consider these players and the considerations applying to them.

The monarch, as head of state and commander-in-chief of the armed services

The normal constitutional position is that, when the appropriate time comes, prime ministers offer their resignation to the monarch, who then asks 'the person who appears most likely to be able to command the confidence of the House to serve as Prime Minister and to form a government' (*Cabinet Manual*, paragraph 2.8). But the scenario we are exploring here is one in which a premier, having lost the confidence of the Commons, does not offer to go. What can the monarch, in such a circumstance, do? In strict legal terms, they possess the power not only to appoint, but to remove a prime minister;* but it has been so long since they used that power that to revive it now would be difficult to contemplate. As the *Manual* recognises (paragraph 2.9):

> Historically, the Sovereign has made use of reserve powers to dismiss a Prime Minister or to make a personal choice of successor, although this was last used in 1834 and was regarded as having undermined the Sovereign.†

As the *Manual* goes on (paragraph 2.9): 'In modern

---

* Gough Whitlam was dismissed as prime minister of Australia in 1975 by the Governor-General.

† When William IV dismissed Lord Melbourne as prime minister despite having a majority in the House of Commons.

times the convention has been that the Sovereign should not be drawn into party politics'. In this sense, there is a strong convention that prime ministers (like other senior politicians) should not behave in a way that puts the monarch in an awkward position, in which they are faced with – on the one hand – allowing an objectionable outcome to come about or continue, or – on the other hand – intervening personally and visibly in politics. The 'limpet' scenario entails a monarch being presented with just such a dilemma by their own prime minister. The Sovereign could on his own initiative use what the *Manual* describes as the 'reserve' powers – by dismissing the Prime Minister or dissolving Parliament, leading to a general election. But either act would be a drastic departure from prevailing understandings, the very bodyguard of the UK's constitutional monarchy. It might be argued that, since the Premier had already broken with convention, then the Monarch was, in turn, released from his obligations on this crucial matter. But it would be a profoundly uncomfortable position for a UK head of state and one he is deeply unlikely to adopt. The 'rogue' Prime Minister's conduct should not – would not – tempt a constitutionally impeccable monarch to behave like a 'rogue' head of state.

But it is established, by custom practice and expectation as first formulated by the political journalist Walter Bagehot in the mid-1860s, that 'the sovereign has, under a constitutional monarchy such as ours, three rights – the right to be consulted, the right to encourage, the right to warn.'[8] It would, then, be in order for the Monarch to find a way of communicating to the Prime Minister that – should they not offer their resignation – there will be consequences. Alongside dismissal or dissolution, a less drastic first step could be for the Monarch to make a public broadcast. If asked – which we have not been – to provide advice on this, the Monarch could make a statement building on his speeches (quoted on pages 6–7) and calling for common sense and respect for the 'precious principles of constitutional government' to prevail.

In the fraught circumstances surrounding this episode, other aspects of the role of the head of state, especially their status as commander-in-chief of the Armed Forces, could come into play. It would not only be the legal authority they possess, but assurance that those serving in such institutions regard their overriding loyalty as being to the monarch, and not to politicians currently in office.

The speaker of the House of Commons

The speaker of the House of Commons has both the responsibility and the capacity to seek to resolve a 'limpet' scenario. *Erskine May: Parliamentary Practice*, the definitive account of parliamentary procedure, describes the speaker as having functions including being 'the spokesperson or representative of the House in its relations with the Crown, the House of Lords and other authorities and persons outside Parliament.' It would, therefore, be proper for the speaker to seek to communicate with the monarch over the issue, so too with the Lords and the outside world – a kind of constitutional postman whose round encompasses the grandest addresses in the Kingdom. Furthermore, they have the ability to prevent the House of Commons from functioning, as a means of pressuring a prime minister who refuses to leave despite having lost the confidence of MPs. As *Erskine May* puts it: 'the Speaker presides over the debates of the House of Commons and enforces the observance of all rules for preserving order in its proceedings.'[9] If they wanted to prevent the Commons from functioning, it would be within their ability to do so.

At a critical point in history, a speaker of the House of Commons (in the English Parliament), William Lenthall, famously resisted executive aggrandisement when, in 1642, Charles I entered the House attempting to arrest five of its members.[10] On this earlier occasion, it was the monarch, Charles I, who was the offending party. In the scenario postulated here, the Speaker might seek to enlist the ruler to deal with problems produced by his own chief minister.

The prime minister and their Cabinet colleagues

A circumstance of the type envisaged here is theoretically possible partly because of the lack of hard constraints upon the power of the prime minister. The system rests upon their recognising when it is time for them to leave and offering their resignation accordingly. But while a prime minister might be able to exploit the informality surrounding their powers, it can also work against them. Much of the authority to act within the government, for instance, rests not with the premier but with other ministers in the government. The prime minister cannot order them to act. Therefore, in circumstances in which they deliberately depart from convention in ways that suit them, might such behaviour, in turn, weaken them in other ways? If, for instance, other members of their government became uncertain about their project, they could refuse to assist them in pursuing it. A chancellor of the Exchequer, for example, might choose not to use their power to impose courses of action upon the Bank of England intended to deal with problems in the financial markets, which can be the most potent force of all in trumping political outcomes.

Other ministers might regard a prime minister trying to 'do the wrong thing', as they might see it, with great anxiety. For example, a lord chancellor, who has sworn a personal oath to uphold the rule of law, might be persuadable to 'do the right thing', either by their own consciences or by individual defenders of the constitution in Crown service. A prime minister could in theory remove an obstructive Cabinet member, or they might resign. But somebody more compliant would need to be found in their place – although in theory government can continue to function even if key posts are unfilled. Furthermore, as already discussed, it is only by convention that various royal prerogative powers, upon which much prime-ministerial authority rests, are at the disposal of the premier.[11] A circumstance in which the usual constitutional understandings are being ignored could make it more plausible that a monarch might feel able to resist their prime minister in deploying the prerogatives. If the premier ceases to act as a 'good chap', then the monarch might do so also. Though the current sovereign strikes us as being thoroughly doused in the 'theory'.

The leaders of the anti-authoritarian parties

It would be entirely within constitutional norms for leaders of parties outside the existing government to discuss and press for the formation of a new administration. They need not be simple bystanders. As the *Cabinet Manual* explains, following a general election which produces no single-party majority (paragraph 2.9):

> it is the responsibility of those involved in the political process, and in particular the parties represented in Parliament, to seek to determine and communicate clearly to the Sovereign who is best placed to be able to command the confidence of the House of Commons.

It continues (paragraph 2.13):

> Where a range of different administrations could potentially be formed, political parties may wish to hold discussions to establish who is best able to

command the confidence of the House of Commons
and should form the next government.

Parliament, including the House of Lords

This episode would in some ways be a clash between
Parliament, including its elected component, the
Commons, and the executive, or at least its political
leadership. Key levers possessed by the Commons (if
operating) would include the ability to vote on motions,
most obviously a no-confidence motion. The Commons
could block or refuse to confirm legislative measures
(including delegated as well as primary legislation), and
also withhold supply – that is, money – from the government. It might take time for such a measure to become
directly effective, and a government could seek to borrow
on the markets if denied fiscal support. But, given the
nature of contemporary finance, the money markets
would surely move very swiftly against the rogue government, adding powerfully to the financial, economic, and
political instability in which the limpet administration
would be striving to operate.

While the Commons would be on the front line, the
Lords would be likely still to play a part, and the speakers
of both chambers would be advised to remain in close
contact. This scenario assumes a majority opposed to the
limpet Prime Minister. But if, for some reason, a majority were secured in the Commons for the passing of an
objectionable legal measure, the Lords has the power by
law to delay it by around a year or – if it comprised an

attempt to extend the length of a Parliament beyond five years – to veto it absolutely. If in agreement, the Commons and Lords between them might, for instance, pass emergency legislation addressed to the problem of the squatter Prime Minister clinging on in Downing Street, to present for royal assent.

Both chambers and individuals within them could use their reputational power to create pressure. There would be value in their considering the use of novel parliamentary measures, such as changes to standing orders for particular purposes. There might also be interest in reviving older practices. For instance, the House of Commons could in theory punish – and possibly detain – an MP for contempt. However, such proceedings are difficult to reconcile with contemporary legal expectations and standards and are probably obsolete.[12]

The chief of the defence staff

The chief of the defence staff is the prime minister's principal military adviser. Should a prime minister seek to deploy the Armed Forces in a way intended to maintain their position, the chief of the defence staff and their personal robustness would be tested. They report to the secretary of state for defence and the prime minister, but are appointed by the monarch. Were the CDS to seek to resist particular courses of action, the position of the head of state could, once again, be important to their success (or lack of) in doing so. The legislature also has a potential role here in that, under the Bill of Rights, the maintenance of the armed services without the annual approval of Parliament is illegal.

In 2000, Sir Frank Cooper, an outstanding figure in Whitehall and a former permanent secretary of the Ministry of Defence, made a particular point to one of the authors (PH), in the course of an on-the-record conversation about the UK's arrangements for nuclear release, that a constitutional safeguard existed lest a prime minister lost judgement and tried to issue an order for a nuclear strike for which his or her CDS thought there was no military justification.

This is how the conversation ran:

HENNESSY: Can I ask you a question which tends to lurk in people's minds about this? What if a Prime Minister went bananas … at a period of high international tension and authorised the release of the British nuclear weapon, and the military advisers concerned, and those small groups of civil servants who were involved as well, realised that the prime minister was crackers – what would happen?

COOPER: Well, the key word is 'authorised'. The Prime Minister can only authorise the use of force or the use of nuclear weapons or anything of that kind, he cannot give an order. The only legitimate orders can be given by commissioned officers of Her Majesty's Forces. And this is a fine distinction but not unimportant.

HENNESSY: So, what would happen if I was Prime

Minister and you were my Chief of the Defence Staff and I said 'Frank, I authorise the use of the British nuclear weapon', and you thought I was bananas? What would you do?

COOPER: Well, I'd argue with the Prime Minister for some time. ... I'd certainly argue with him and, in the last analysis, say: 'Well, I'm not going to do that' – which would probably mean you'd get court martialled if you survived. But it may be totally against your military judgement. Now the Prime Minister's response to that would be to fire me straight away and get a more pliant officer.

Sir Frank went on to explain that 'this distinction between authorisation and the power to give orders is a very important one ... this is where you are into the royal prerogative basically. And, you know, there are many, many cases where the royal prerogative actually plays a very useful part in life and if you didn't have it you *would* need a written constitution.'[13]

We are not suggesting that there could be a nuclear element to any 'limpet prime minister' crisis, but the Cooper testimony is worth including as an example of the constitutional aspects of the PM/CDS relationship: not least because it illustrates how at least one very senior figure in post-war Whitehall *had* given thought and attention to the most ghastly contingency of them all.

The cabinet secretary

The cabinet secretary has a variety of important roles supporting the prime minister and collective government, and as head of the Civil Service, they are the official leader of the administrative machine. In the circumstances generated by our 'limpet prime minister' scenario, the cabinet secretary is an absolutely crucial figure. Almost all of the wiring – hidden or in plain sight – runs across their desk. The extent to which they are able to resist or influence events could be critical. While, ultimately, they are obliged to loyally support the ministers they serve (or resign from their posts), cabinet secretaries are also required to bring relevant information to the attention of those ministers, even if inconvenient from the point of view of those with whom they are communicating. The cabinet secretary has an important role in nearly all constitutional matters. At the heart of the job lies the guardianship of the constitution. In fact, they might be seen as the permanent secretary for the constitution. With the private secretary to the monarch and the principal private secretary to the prime minister, they comprise the 'Golden Triangle'.[14] This communication network is responsible for overseeing and choreographing the most sensitive of constitutional operations, and we might expect it to be active and vital during our 'limpet' episode.

The cabinet secretary must, for example, seek to promote and act upon certain core principles included in the *Cabinet Manual*, such as the previously cited stipulation that when the confidence of the Commons has been lost, and an alternative administration appears to exist, the prime minister should resign. During a period in which the government seems to lack the confidence of the Commons, the cabinet secretary might also seek to impress upon the prime minister (perhaps with little success) the need to adhere to certain restraints. The *Manual* notes that (paragraph 2.16):

> As long as there is significant doubt following an election over the Government's ability to command the confidence of the House of Commons, certain restrictions on government activity apply ...

The *Manual* goes on (paragraph 2.27):

> While the government retains its responsibility to govern and ministers remain in charge of their departments, governments are expected by convention to observe discretion in initiating any new action of a continuing or long-term character in the period immediately preceding an election, immediately afterwards if the result is unclear, and following the loss of a vote of confidence.

Principles a cabinet secretary might try to assert include those set out in paragraph 2.29 of the *Manual*, referring to the need for 'deferral of activity such as: taking or announcing major policy decisions; entering into large/contentious procurement contracts or significant long-term commitments; and making some senior public appointments and approving Senior Civil Service appointments'.

The *Manual* suggests a role for the cabinet secretary in cross-party government formation processes. Paragraph 2.13 states that:

> Where a range of different administrations could potentially be formed, political parties may wish to hold discussions to establish who is best able to command the confidence of the House of Commons and should form the next government. The Sovereign would not expect to become involved in any negotiations, although there are responsibilities on those involved in the process to keep the Palace informed. This could be done by political parties or the Cabinet Secretary. The Principal Private Secretary to the Prime Minister may also have a role, for example, in communicating with the Palace.

This paragraph seems to open up possibilities for the cabinet secretary, though the incumbent prime minister might not want them to utilise them.

If, as would be likely, the 'limpet' scenario had been preceded by years of corrosion in official/ministerial relationships, with the tacit understandings being progressively swept aside by a growing tide of what Lord

Hailsham famously called an 'elective dictatorship',* the crucial fabric between the job of prime minister and that of cabinet secretary is likely to have already experienced a serious rending. However august a figure the cabinet secretary might be, waving the *Cabinet Manual* and the *Ministerial Code* across the table at a prime minister might not arouse the feelings of respect and acceptance on which their successful functioning depends. With words of resentful fantasy about an alleged 'deep state' or a 'blob' of silky-smooth mandarins seeking to defang a radical government at every turn, 'enemies of the people', no less, in collusive yet unspoken alliance against the government's wishes with the senior judiciary. For a certain sort of minister, convenient, all-explaining conspiracy theories have a real attraction and are a permanent temptation for those who think in the primary colours of fantasy rather than the more complicated pastel shades of reality. And every row or ruptured relationship reinforces the stone-cladding of the aggrieved premier's conviction that the staff cannot be trusted.

One of the jobs once included in the cabinet secretary's portfolio of functions was adviser on defence and foreign policy, with oversight of the budgets of the secret world. In more recent times those have been hived off to a

---

* Hailsham, in his 1976 Dimbleby Lecture, made this phrase famous when referring to the lack of constitutional restraints, under the 'unwritten' or 'uncodified' UK model, applying to a group with a majority in the House of Commons.

national security adviser. However, the cabinet secretary has regained the role of accounting officer for the Single Intelligence Account – a function that could potentially become significant to efforts to restrain a rogue prime minister.[15] They might also provide some degree of discreet support to a director-general of the Security Service choosing to initiate an investigation into possible foreign links on the part of the prime minister.

The judiciary

The Supreme Court has already acted as the last line of defence against a rogue prime minister, when in September 2019 it ruled unlawful the attempted prorogation of Parliament by Boris Johnson. It is virtually certain that, while political events were playing out around a 'limpet', one or more legal challenges, perhaps crowdfunded, would be mounted, aimed at restricting or dislodging the Prime Minister. It is difficult to predict the precise form they would take and how far the courts would entertain them. But it is possible that the courts – as they did during the years following the EU referendum of 2016 – would become a focus for controversy, and their resolve would be tested. Both the monarch and Parliament could offer protection for the judiciary in 'limpet' circumstances, since – under Article VII of the 1701 Act of Settlement – the removal of judges can take place only with the agreement of both Houses of Parliament.

A handful of very senior officers in the secret services

Among this group, the individual whose statutory and constitutional role (previously discussed in relation to the Security Service Act 1989) might make them well-placed to seek to uphold good practice is the director-general of the Security Service.

The permanent secretary to the Treasury

Within government, the permanent secretary to the Treasury (the supplier of government finances) could promote principles of the type set out in paragraph 2.29 of the *Cabinet Manual*. In its discussion of circumstances in which the government lacks a Commons majority, it calls for 'the deferral of activity such as ... entering into large/contentious procurement contracts or significant long-term commitments.' Also, the sum of money required daily just to maintain the apparatus of government is huge and every tranche has to be signed off by the Treasury. Other permanent secretaries could be involved; for example, the Home Office permanent secretary traditionally has a lot to do with the Palace and an intimate association with MI5.

The governor of the Bank of England

It seems inevitable that some degree of market instability, possibly of increasing intensity, would accompany this scenario. Another office holder at the head of a key public institution would, therefore, face a dilemma. The governor of the Bank of England (the government's lender of last resort) might, on the one hand, wish to take steps to minimise economic and financial damage to the country. But, on the other hand, to do so might be to insulate and effectively further the constitutionally improper objectives of the recalcitrant Prime Minister. In deciding how they respond to this scenario, the governor will be aware that they are accountable for their actions to Parliament.

More details of the constitutional landscape can be found in the *Memorandum of Understanding on Resolution Planning and Financial Crisis Management*, agreed between the Bank and the Treasury and presented to Parliament in 2017, in accordance with the Financial Services Act 2012. It states (paragraph 38) that:

The Bank has primary responsibility for financial stability and operational responsibility for managing financial crises. But consistent with the Treasury's overall responsibilities, the Chancellor may, in some circumstances during a financial crisis, use additional powers to direct the Bank. This is provided for in Section 61 of the [Financial Services] Act, which allows the Chancellor to direct the Bank to:
- conduct special support operations for the financial system as whole, in operations going beyond the Bank's published frameworks;
- provide ELA [Emergency Liquidity Assistance] in a support operation going beyond the Bank's

published frameworks to one or more firms that
are not judged by the Bank to be solvent and
viable;

- provide ELA in a support operation going
beyond the Bank's published frameworks to
one or more firms on terms other than those
proposed by the Bank; and
- implement a particular SRR [Special Resolution
Regime] stabilisation option.

These provisions were not devised with a financial
crisis triggered by a limpet prime minister in mind. But
in such circumstances, if the governor was reluctant
to act, in effect, to shore up what they regarded as an
illegitimate administration, the chancellor would – in
accordance with the memorandum – be able to override them and order that action be taken. This scenario
assumes that the chancellor of the Exchequer is committed to maintaining their prime minister in office.
It also relies on the most senior Bank personnel being
compliant.

The comptroller and auditor general

The comptroller and auditor general is the official
ensurer that the government spends money only
accordance with the express wishes of Parliament. Any
expenditure by a limpet government would be of questionable legitimacy. Embarking on new programmes,
perhaps intended to build and/or maintain bases of

support within Parliament and on the outside, would be a dubious practice and a break with proper procedure in the context of a government that lacked the confidence of the Commons. It is plausible that a prime minister in this scenario would also be pursuing practices in the use of public money that were more obviously corrupt. The comptroller and auditor general, who is head of the National Audit Office, is an office-holder independent of government and attached to Parliament, and as such could potentially play a part in supporting Parliament in any efforts to restrain the prime minister. The Budget Responsibility and National Audit Act 2011 (Section 11) stipulates that the monarch appoints them on the recommendation of the prime minister, but who must have the agreement of the chair of the Committee of Public Accounts (a post held by an opposition MP). Section 12 of the Act explains that the comptroller is 'an officer of the House of Commons' and that:

(3) The person who is Comptroller and Auditor General may not be a member of the House of Lords.
(4) The Comptroller and Auditor General is not to be regarded—
   (a) as the servant or agent of the Crown, or
   (b) as enjoying any status, immunity or privilege of the Crown.
(5) The person who is Comptroller and Auditor General may not hold any other office or position to

which a person may be appointed, or recommended for appointment, by or on behalf of the Crown.

These provisions underpin the principle that the comptroller and auditor general is attached to Parliament, and not the executive, and is therefore independent of a premier seeking to retain control of the government.

The clerk of the House of Commons

The clerk of the House of Commons, as head of the House service, has operational control of all that is necessary for the House of Commons to sit and transact business. They also act as accounting officer for the House Vote and take personal responsibility for the propriety of House of Commons expenditure, so they could not authorise activities associated with limpetry. The Speaker would consult closely with them on steps to be taken in such a circumstance.

Next steps

We have sketched out the considerations applying to some of the main constitutional players. But given the complex interplay of people and uncertain powers, and the silence of existing conventions about this contingency, it is difficult to predict with certainty what would fall where on the scales. What *is* apparent from this overview of the mechanisms and the individual office-holders that might protect democracy in dire – and we hope never-to-emerge – circumstances is that, while there are some lines of defence, they might be more clearly defined and aligned. There is room for improvement. Recent experiences have provided a warning about the vulner-abilities of our system. It would be too easy to conclude that we have passed through the worst and it is time to move on from worrying about constitutional disasters.

We believe, however, that now that we have a stable government enjoying a very substantial majority in the House of Commons we can take a rounded view of our democratic defence installations, their strengths and weaknesses, and possible improvements. The contin-gency we are contemplating, should the authoritarian squatters in Downing Street prevail, would bite deep and hard into the 'living nerve' of the nation's political and constitutional consciousness.[16] If our politicians got this crisis wrong and our constitution failed to take the strain, our long-established ruling assumptions would lose their sway. We would be a very different country on the other side of it. There would be no disguising the enormity of what had happened either at home or abroad.

There has long been a largely unspoken school of con-stitutional thought in the United Kingdom which main-tains that in ambiguity lies flexibility and, therefore, strength. The authors have never been persuaded by this example of British exceptionalism. We are wholly uncon-vinced of its assumptions and characteristics today.

To forethink is to be forearmed. Our sole proposal, therefore, is simple and uncluttered: the creation of

a Committee of Privy Counsellors to examine the
long-term resilience, protection, and preservation
of British parliamentary democracy.

Such a committee could take evidence in both public
and private before reaching a judgement about the ade-
quacy of the mixture of statutes, codes, procedures, and tacit
understandings that, together, comprise our protections. It
would report to the speakers of both Houses of Parliament.
As much of its text as possible would be published.

The width of the trawl of information sought for this
stretching task would be up to them. From our point of
view, the priority is that the committee should be con-
vened and that it should be fuelled by an acute sense of
urgency and importance. While the precise approach it
took to its task would be a matter for the Committee
and those commissioning it, we make some initial sug-
gestions here. It might:

- Attempt a broad definition of our democratic
  system and the key elements that must be
  preserved if it is to retain its integrity, perhaps
  like the one we proposed earlier in this work.
- Assess the threats to this model. They might
  include populist movements, terrorist groups,
  or organised entities falling slightly short of
  being defined as terrorists. There would need to
  be discussion of hostile international powers,
  including both states and other actors.

- Consider the range of potential tools available to, or being employed by, those who pose these threats – and those who support them – and technologies such as social media.
- Assess the extent to which present challenges are a new departure, and if so the precedents that exist for them and how analogous challenges were addressed in the past. It should draw on the widest range of evidence from history, the social sciences, and elsewhere.
- Discuss a range of scenarios in which such forces, or proxies for them, have or might attain a presence within more established political institutions, including Parliament and the government.
- Create an itinerary of the range of means, including hard laws, conventions, institutions, and people, that can be drawn upon to prevent the emergence of such scenarios, and reverse or at least mitigate them if they came about.
- Consider how far the means available are adequate, and, to the extent they are not, propose additional protections. We do not wish to pre-empt what they might be, but a central theme would likely be means of reenforcing the existing understandings that underpin the system. The Committee might, for instance, seek ways of making confidence (and no-confidence) votes more clearly

binding. We have previously advocated that
incoming premiers should be required to take
an oath in public (in the House of Commons
in the presence of the speaker), committing
themselves to maintenance of constitutional
standards during the term of office.[17] Perhaps
some version of this practice could be useful.
For instance – rather than being made in
Parliament – the oath might be taken in private
to the monarch at the time of a prime minister's
appointment. On our projected 'night of the
limpet', the head of state might be able to
remind their premier of the undertakings they
made on the earlier occasion.

- In doing so, have close regard to the need to
  avoid introducing measures which are a greater
  risk from a democratic standpoint than the
  scenarios which they are intended to address.
  Measures intended to protect democracy can
  be used to unravel it, and we do not wish to
  contribute to such an outcome. However, we
  believe it is important that threats of the type
  we discuss here are considered and addressed in
  a measured way, before they are upon us. It is
  very clear from our inquiries that nothing like
  this has been done in the past or is presently
  contemplated for the future.

Part Three

The Ten-Year Stress Test

The Ten-Year Stress Test traces the events, constitutional developments, and tensions that have beset – one might also say shaken – the UK since the 2014 referendum on Scottish independence. It has been a decade 'crowded with incident', to borrow a phrase from that great (fictional) observer of late Victorian politics, Oscar Wilde's Lady Bracknell.[1] And those 'incidents', at a time of political uncertainty punctuated by upheaval, have tended to be disruptors rather than bringers of stability.

Chronology of a stress test

Scottish independence referendum (18 September 2014): Voters in Scotland supported continued membership of the UK by roughly 55 per cent to 45 per cent. But rather than settling the issue, as advocates of referendums claim they can, the contest made it more salient. In the period since 2014, while subsiding at times, the independence question – and the fraught divisions associated with it – has proved persistent. The referendum was a trigger for expansions in devolution across the UK.

2015 General Election (7 May): The Conservatives

secured a ten-seat majority in the House of Commons on a 36.8 per cent vote share. Their leader, David Cameron, had committed to a negotiation with the EU followed by an in–out referendum on membership.

Jeremy Corbyn's leadership of the Labour Party (12 September 2015–4 April 2020): The Corbyn leadership was associated with various tensions, including between him and his own parliamentary party. This led at times to dysfunction in the official opposition party, making it harder for it to perform its crucial constitutional function.

EU referendum (23 June 2016): During the campaign, collective Cabinet responsibility was formally suspended. In the years that have followed, adherence to this principle has often proved difficult to sustain. A variety of claims have been made about the referendum, involving matters such as the dissemination of false information, the improper use of digital campaigning techniques, and possible foreign interference.

The vote produced a 52 per cent to 48 per cent result in favour of leaving the EU. This outcome triggered a prolonged period of disruption in UK politics. One source of this phenomenon was the uneven dispersal of votes on either side. Scotland and Northern Ireland both produced majorities in favour of remaining but were required to leave along with the whole of the UK. This divergence was a source of territorial destabilisation. The referendum campaign revealed and acerbated divisions over social issues. Those on the 'leave' side tended towards more 'small-c conservative' dispositions. A desire to mobilise this public cleavage seems to have motivated various constitutionally challenging policies subsequently pursued by Conservative governments, including those pertaining to refugees. Efforts to implement the 'leave' result entailed tensions between the executive and Parliament and were connected to controversies about the political role of the courts.

Article 50 *Miller I* law case (October 2016–January 2017): As a consequence of this case, the government was forced to obtain specific statutory authorisation from Parliament before it could trigger Article 50 of the Treaty on European Union to begin the process of exiting the bloc. This case was the occasion for hostile media coverage of courts, part of a wider such tendency. The then lord chancellor and secretary of state for justice, Liz Truss, declined to respond in support of the judiciary.

2017 General Election (8 June): The Conservative Party increased its vote share by 5.5 per cent to 42.3 per cent but lost its overall majority in the House of Commons. The Conservative leader, Theresa May, continued in a minority government with parliamentary support from the Democratic Unionist Party. One of the consequences of this weakened position was the difficulty the Conservative administration faced in securing support for its Brexit deal. In 2019 in particular it suffered a series of defeats in the Commons, unprecedented in their scale and frequency. In the autumn of 2019, a cross-party majority of MPs wrested control of the parliamentary agenda from the executive, imposing legal requirements on the then prime minister, Boris Johnson, in his negotiations with the EU.

Boris Johnson premiership (24 July 2019–6 September 2022): During his period as prime minister, as he had done earlier in his career, Johnson tested constitutional norms in a variety of ways. Looking back, he was a one-man stress test for the British constitution, of a kind it had never experienced before. Even seasoned constitution-watchers were seriously shaken by what he revealed of the flimsiness of the conventions on which we have relied for so long. It was like letting a JCB loose in an area of outstanding natural beauty. Two independent advisers on ministerial interests left their posts during his tenure. Most notoriously, Johnson broke his own lockdown laws by taking part in gatherings at Downing Street. He was subsequently found by a parliamentary inquiry to have knowingly misled Parliament over this subject, and it was concluded that he and his allies had sought to undermine its work. A further scandal involving an inappropriate ministerial appointment and the dissemination of false information brought about the end of Johnson's term of office.

Attempted prorogation of Parliament and *Miller II* law case (August–September 2019): The Johnson government sought to prevent Parliament from meeting for a period in the lead-up to the projected exit from the EU on 31 October. This attempt was found unlawful by the Supreme Court, which ruled that Parliament must reconvene to continue to hold the government to account. The judiciary was once again drawn into the centre of heightened political controversy.

Pandemic and lockdown (January 2020–March 2022): Covid-19 produced a variety of constitutional tensions, testing emergency response mechanisms in new ways. Intensifying a pre-existing tendency that can be traced back at least as far as the 1920s, the government relied heavily on delegated legislation, bringing about major restrictions on the freedom of the public through measures not subject to full public scrutiny.

During this period, the usual rules regarding processes for the awarding of public contracts to private-sector companies were relaxed. Practices followed and decisions made, often involving considerable sums of money, have become the subject of intense critical scrutiny.

EU–UK Trade and Cooperation Agreement (came into force 1 May 2021): This agreement had expansive implications for the UK across a number of fields. One significant constitutional aspect involved Northern Ireland and measures contained within it to preclude a hard border in the island of Ireland. The UK government proved reluctant to abide fully by the agreement it had reached, even to the point of contemplating the deliberate violation of international law. This issue was an ongoing source of strain for EU–UK relations, which somewhat lessened following the coming into effect of the 2023 Windsor Framework. It was also connected to pronounced difficulties with the peace process and the functioning of power-sharing arrangements in the territory.

Liz Truss premiership (6 September–25 October 2022): The extent to which Truss could ever have been said to have clearly commanded the confidence of the House of Commons is questionable. She took office after a Conservative leadership contest in which she failed to come first in any of the rounds of votes by her own MPs, but won among the wider party membership. Her premiership itself was short but eventful, including from a constitutional perspective. Notable events included the immediate displacement of the permanent secretary to the Treasury, Tom Scholar. Truss's government sought to implement major changes in fiscal policy while bypassing more regular oversight processes. It was marked by strains to the principle of collective responsibility, with differences between Cabinet members manifesting themselves publicly.

Death of Elizabeth II and accession of Charles III (September 2022): The transition from one monarch to the next was a test to constitutional arrangements in that it was the first such transfer since 1952. It appeared to take place smoothly.

An audit of disturbance and stability

First, the 2014 referendum itself and the 2016 vote on the UK's continued membership of the European Union. Put aside for a moment the outcomes and the consequences; the referendum ballots have shown how uneasily a plebiscitary system sits alongside our dominant democratic mode of representative democracy conducted through general elections, in a way that could not have been predicted during and after the 1975 referendum on our continued membership of what was then the European Economic Community (which was conducted in a generally decorous manner and produced a two-thirds to one-third vote in favour of remaining). By contrast, each of the 2014 and 2016 referendum campaigns drew on wells of venom, the poison from which has not wholly dissipated in their aftermath.

Referendums do not sit well with our party system either. But the European question has created pressure to hold them, for it has never slid naturally into our standard model for resolving disputes of Left/Right divisions through general elections and tussles in the House of Commons. If referendums have now established themselves as our instrument of choice for settling constitutional disputes that the standard model cannot handle, that, of itself, would represent a huge change and a bringer of heat in a country calling out for light.

In our judgement, the matter of referendums towers over any of the other constitutional questions that have freckled the years since 2014. As follows are the others caught up in the net of our constitutional trawl.

Behavioural and procedural matters
The following paragraphs consider rules and standards applying to government, the behaviour of people within

the relevant institutions, and the interactions between them.

Adherence to the 'Nolan Principles' of standards in public life

The Seven Principles of Public Life, first promulgated in May 1995, are:

1.1 Selflessness: Holders of public office should act solely in terms of the public interest.

1.2 Integrity: Holders of public office must avoid placing themselves under any obligation to people or organisations that might try inappropriately to influence them in their work. They should not act or take decisions in order to gain financial or other material benefits for themselves, their family, or their friends. They must declare and resolve any interests and relationships.

1.3 Objectivity: Holders of public office must act and take decisions impartially, fairly and on merit, using the best evidence and without discrimination or bias.

1.4 Accountability: Holders of public office are accountable to the public for their decisions and actions and must submit themselves to the scrutiny necessary to ensure this.

1.5 Openness: Holders of public office should act and take decisions in an open and transparent manner. Information should not be withheld from the public unless there are clear and lawful reasons for so doing.

1.6 Honesty: Holders of public office should be truthful.

1.7 Leadership: Holders of public office should exhibit these principles in their own behaviour and treat others with respect. They should actively promote and robustly support the principles and challenge poor behaviour wherever it occurs.[2]

We have previously measured the performance of Boris Johnson as prime minister and his government against these seven principles and identified doubts about compliance.[3] Further evidence of such failings, both under Johnson and his successors, have surfaced since our previous assessment, conducted in mid-2022. For example, the House of Commons Committee of Privileges, investigating whether Johnson had committed a contempt in the way he responded to questions about lockdown gatherings, concluded in June 2023 that he had set out:

to undermine the parliamentary process, by:
a) Deliberately misleading the House
b) Deliberately misleading the Committee
c) Breaching confidence
d) Impugning the Committee and thereby undermining the democratic process of the House
e) Being complicit in the campaign of abuse and attempted intimidation of the Committee.[4]

The improper behaviour extended beyond Johnson himself and to other senior politicians. Later in the month, the Committee issued another report dealing with this matter, in which it expressed:

> our concern at the improper pressure brought to bear on the Committee and its members throughout this inquiry. We are concerned in particular at the involvement of Members of both Houses in attempting to influence the outcome of the inquiry. Those Members did not choose to engage through any proper process such as the submission of letters or evidence to our inquiry, but by attacking the members of the Committee, in order to influence their judgement. Their aim was to (1) influence the outcome of the inquiry, (2) impede the work of the Committee by inducing members to resign from it, (3) discredit the Committee's conclusions if those conclusions were not what they wanted, and (4) discredit the Committee as a whole.[5]

During this episode, a number of senior public figures – including the Prime Minister – had exhibited behaviour that departed significantly from the standards associated with the Seven Principles, not least those of honesty and leadership, and did so in a way that became widely, publicly visible.

Disregard for the conventions of collective Cabinet responsibility

The *Cabinet Manual* (introduction to Chapter 4) states that:

> Cabinet and Cabinet committees take decisions which are binding on members of the Government. Cabinet and Cabinet committees are composed of government ministers, who are then accountable to Parliament for any collective decisions made. Collective responsibility allows ministers to express their views frankly in discussion, in the expectation that they can maintain a united front once a decision has been reached.

The *Ministerial Code* (paragraph 5.3) stipulates:

> The internal process through which a decision has been made, or the level of Committee by which it was taken should not be disclosed. Neither should the individual views of Ministers or advice provided by civil servants as part of that internal process be disclosed. Decisions reached by the Cabinet or Ministerial Committees are binding on all members of the Government.

It adds (paragraph 8.3) that:

> Ministers should ensure that their statements are

consistent with collective Government policy. Ministers should take special care in referring to subjects which are the responsibility of other Ministers.

There is evidence of government ministers showing increasing willingness to break ranks publicly from their colleagues. When foreign secretary under Theresa May, Johnson publicly promoted ideas about his favoured approach to Brexit, which appeared to depart from agreed policy.[6] A later case of an open breakdown in Cabinet solidarity came during the Truss premiership. As the difficulties of this administration intensified, ministers who appeared to diverge or distance themselves from established positions and decisions taken included even Truss herself. When asked, in a BBC interview on 2 October 2022, about whether the whole of the Cabinet were aware of the intention of removing the highest rate of income tax, Truss – still serving as prime minister at the time – replied:

> No, no we didn't. It was a decision that the chancellor made ... When budgets are developed, they are developed in a very confidential way. They are very market sensitive. Of course, the cabinet is briefed, but it is never the case on budgets that they are created by the whole cabinet.[7]

When Suella Braverman was finally removed from the Cabinet in November 2023, it was after, as home secretary, repeatedly making public statements – over immigration, homelessness, and policing of demonstrations – that seemed to amount to departures from collective responsibility.[8]

Recklessness in the deployment of executive powers

One example of this is the use of the royal prerogative to prorogue Parliament. Boris Johnson sought, in the late summer and early autumn of 2019, to prevent Parliament from meeting during part of the period leading up to the projected exit date of the UK from the EU. A legal challenge followed. The Supreme Court concluded that Johnson had gone beyond what was democratically proper:

> Let us remind ourselves of the foundations of our constitution. We live in a representative democracy. The House of Commons exists because the people have elected its members. The Government is not directly elected by the people (unlike the position in some other democracies). The Government exists because it has the confidence of the House of Commons. It has no democratic legitimacy other than that. This means that it is accountable to the House of Commons – and indeed to the House of Lords – for its actions, remembering always that the actual task of governing is for the executive and not for Parliament or the courts.

Having set out this general democratic principle, the Court then considered its application in the specific context of the attempted prorogation:

> The first question, therefore, is whether the Prime Minister's action had the effect of frustrating or preventing the constitutional role of Parliament in holding the Government to account ... The answer is that of course it did ... Such an interruption in the process of responsible government might not matter in some circumstances. But the circumstances here were, as already explained, quite exceptional ... It is impossible for us to conclude, on the evidence which has been put before us, that there was any reason – let alone a good reason – to advise Her Majesty to prorogue Parliament for five weeks, from 9th or 12th September until 14th October. We cannot speculate, in the absence of further evidence, upon what such reasons might have been. It follows that the decision was unlawful.[9]

The Court, then, was upholding democracy in the face of improper executive action.

Lack of respect for processes intended to maintain probity and uphold constitutional standards

A number of senior politicians have been forced out of office by official inquiries that have found them to have departed from acceptable standards. But even though exiting their posts, they have questioned the processes involved.

In April 2023, after an investigation into his behaviour towards officials identified poor behaviour on his part and forced him to leave the government, Dominic Raab wrote in a public letter to the prime minister, Rishi Sunak, that:

> Whilst I feel duty bound to accept the outcome of the inquiry, it dismissed all but two of the claims levelled against me. I also believe that its two adverse findings are flawed and set a dangerous precedent for the conduct of good government ... In setting the threshold for bullying so low, this inquiry has set a dangerous precedent. It will encourage spurious complaints against ministers, and have a chilling effect on those driving change on behalf of your government – and ultimately the British people.[10]

Johnson resigned as an MP in June 2023. He did so in advance of the House of Commons Committee of Privileges report on the findings of an inquiry into whether he had held the House in contempt when responding to questions about gatherings during the Covid lockdown. Johnson alleged that the Committee had been:

> determined to use the proceedings against me to drive me out of Parliament. They have still not

produced a shred of evidence that I knowingly or recklessly misled the Commons ... I did not lie, and I believe that in their hearts, the Committee know it. But they have wilfully chosen to ignore the truth ... Their purpose from the beginning has been to find me guilty, regardless of the facts. This is the very definition of a kangaroo court ... I am not alone in thinking that there is a witch hunt under way, to take revenge for Brexit and ultimately to reverse the 2016 referendum result.

According to Johnson, his own 'removal' was:

the necessary first step, and I believe there has been a concerted attempt to bring it about ... The Privileges Committee is there to protect the privileges of Parliament. That is a very important job. They should not be using their powers – which have only been very recently designed – to mount what is plainly a political hit job on someone they oppose ... I am bewildered and appalled that I can be forced out, anti-democratically, by a committee chaired and managed, by [Labour MP] Harriet Harman, with such egregious bias.[11]

The alleged creeping politicisation of the career Civil Service, and the more overt and widespread politicisation of public appointments

The *Civil Service code* explains the 'core values' of their profession in the following terms:

- 'integrity' is putting the obligations of public service above your own personal interests
- 'honesty' is being truthful and open
- 'objectivity' is basing your advice and decisions on rigorous analysis of the evidence
- 'impartiality' is acting solely according to the merits of the case and serving equally well governments of different political persuasions[12]

Relative security of tenure is important to an individual being about to fulfil these values. However, recent years have seen a considerable number of abrupt departures at highest level in the permanent Civil Service. As the House of Lords Select Committee on the Constitution (of which one of the present authors is a former member) recorded in 2023:

Several recent departures of very senior civil servants have been controversial. In 2020, 12 permanent secretaries or civil servants of equivalent seniority left their posts, including the Cabinet Secretary, Sir Mark Sedwill. In September 2022, Treasury Permanent Secretary Sir Tom Scholar left his post on the day that Rt Hon Elizabeth Truss MP became Prime Minister and Rt Hon Kwasi Kwarteng MP became Chancellor of the Exchequer. This was widely reported as a sacking, in an attempt to move economic policy away from 'Treasury orthodoxy'. In a statement issued at the time, Sir Tom said: 'The Chancellor decided it was time for new leadership at the Treasury.' On the same day, Sir Stephen Lovegrove moved to a new role from that as national Security Adviser, a move also described as a sacking.[13]

Raab's resignation letter to Rishi Sunak from the same year was suggestive of a troubled relationship between some ministers and their officials in the post-2016 era. It also demonstrated such an approach might not be conducive to civil servants drawing attention to important but awkward information, as they are constitutionally required to do (the *Civil Service code* states that 'You must not ... ignore inconvenient facts or relevant considerations when providing advice or making decisions'[14]). Raab wrote that:

> ministers must be able to exercise direct oversight with respect to senior officials over critical negotiations conducted on behalf of the British people, otherwise the democratic and constitutional principle of ministerial responsibility will be lost ... ministers must be able to give direct critical feedback on briefings and submissions to senior officials, in order to set the standards and drive the reform the public expect of us ... I am genuinely sorry for any unintended stress or offence that any officials felt, as a result of the pace, standards and challenge that I brought to the Ministry of Justice. That is, however, what the public expect of ministers working on their behalf ...

I raised with you a number of improprieties that came to light during the course of this inquiry. They include the systematic leaking of skewed and fabricated claims to the media in breach of the rules of the inquiry and the Civil Service Code of Conduct, and the coercive removal by a senior official of dedicated private secretaries from my Ministry of Justice private office ...[15]

This letter suggests deep mistrust on the part of Raab towards officials, and a sense on his part that he had been found to have behaved improperly simply for expecting them to perform.

Anxieties induced by shifts in the wider political culture

These passages deal with broad and deep constitutional, political, and social developments, extending beyond the inner workings of the executive.

Pressure on adherence to the rule of law, both domestic and international

The rule of law rests, among other foundations, upon the courts being able to operate independently without undue external influence; upon their being able to oversee the activities of government, to ensure their legality; and upon international agreements and standards being adhered to. The judiciary has come under pronounced political pressure in recent years, for example for its supposed resistance to the implementation of the outcome of the 2016 EU referendum. When the High Court found against the government in the Article 50 case in November 2016, criticism of them – which the then lord chancellor, Liz Truss, refused directly to rebut – included the notorious 'Enemies of the People' *Daily Mail* headline and story. As part of a wider tendency towards the denigration of public institutions, legal professionals have been targeted by senior politicians, including Suella Braverman. As home secretary, when speaking to the Conservative Party Conference of October 2022 about her asylum policy, Braverman discussed the different groups who might oppose it, remarking: 'As for the lawyers. Don't get me started on the lawyers. And I'm a recovering lawyer.'[16] The particular initiative Braverman was outlining on this occasion was the plan to transport refugees to Rwanda. In pursuit of this objective, the government introduced measures that were challenging both to the domestic rule of law, seeking to minimise the role of the courts in exercising oversight, and were also in tension with treaty obligations and norms of international law. The UK flirted with similar violations of the latter type during the early 2020s with respect to the Northern Ireland Protocol of the EU Withdrawal Agreement.

Excessive use of secondary legislation

The creation and use of delegated powers has long been a source of constitutional concern. They entail ministers and others being able to change the law and – under so-called 'Henry VIII powers' – even alter Acts of Parliament, without being subject to the kind of oversight that might apply to bills passing through Parliament. Parliament can be asked to create these powers without being given a clear idea of the use to which they will be put. These worries have intensified in the context of measures taken in relation first to Brexit and second to the pandemic, arguably bringing about a qualitative change in practice which has spread beyond these specific areas.

The following passages set out the difficulties identified by the Hansard Society with the use of statutory instruments (SIs) in the UK in a November 2021 publication:

Problems with the powers
- The powers given to Ministers to make delegated legislation are frequently too broad.
- Too many Bills are now 'skeleton' Bills that contain powers rather than policy and so cannot be properly scrutinised by Parliament.
- The boundary between what should go in primary legislation and what should go in delegated legislation is blurred.
- When Parliament accepts controversial powers in a Bill, it creates a precedent that makes it politically easier for the government to argue in favour of taking similar powers in subsequent

Bills – creating a 'normalisation' or 'ratchet' effect.

- Broad powers can be used in the future in unexpected ways that Parliament did not anticipate at the time it granted them.
- 'Henry VIII powers' – which enable Ministers to amend or repeal primary legislation by SI – are common, despite their potential for serious constitutional implications.

Problems with the scrutiny of Statutory Instruments
- There is no sensible correlation between the content of an SI and the scrutiny procedure to which it is subject.
- Parliament has no power of amendment, and the risk of an SI being rejected is negligible.
- Government control of the House of Commons agenda restricts MPs' ability to secure debate on SIs of concern.
- Scrutiny procedures are superficial and often a waste of time, particularly in the House of Commons.
- There is no penalty for poor-quality explanatory memoranda and other supporting documentation.
- The system and its terminology are confusing and overly complex.[17]

Also in November 2021, the House of Lords

Secondary Legislation Scrutiny Committee issued a report, *Government by Diktat: A call to return power to Parliament,* containing 'a stark warning – that the balance of power between Parliament and government has for some time been shifting away from Parliament, a trend accentuated by the twin challenges of Brexit and the COVID-19 pandemic.'[18] Working in concert with the Secondary Legislation Scrutiny Committee, another House of Lords body, the Delegated Powers and Regulatory Reform Committee, published *Democracy Denied? The urgent need to rebalance power between Parliament and the Executive*. It referred to 'a disturbing trend in the way in which bills are framed with the effect that they often limit or even avoid appropriate legislative scrutiny ... The shift of power from Parliament to the executive must stop'.[19]

The spread of devices such as WhatsApp in official communication and the partial usurpation of proper Whitehall record-keeping

Increasingly, people within government make use of forms of communication including WhatsApp, self-deleting messages, and personal email addresses (non-corporate communication channels, or NCCCs). They provide for a degree of informality that might detract from adherence to proper procedure, and reduce the degree of accountability for important decision-making. In particular, they can be a vehicle for the exercise of undisclosed external influence on outcomes. In May

2024 the House of Commons Public Administration and Constitutional Affairs Committee noted that:

> The ongoing public inquiry into the Government's COVID-19 response highlights the ubiquity of WhatsApp and other NCCCs in government. A huge volume of messages has been released to the inquiry or, in some cases, has gone missing. The Institute for Government has commented that it would be unwise and unpractical to ban Ministers and Officials from communicating by means of NCCCs. While we heard no calls for such a ban, we do note the comments of a former Director of GCHQ, Sir David Ormand, that their use is entirely unsuited to proper policy making ... evidence submitted to our inquiry revealed clear concern that the lack of disclosure could allow significant lobbying efforts to take place outside the transparency requirements ...
>
> If WhatsApp and other Non-Corporate Communication Channels ('NCCCs') are to be used in government and, in particular, if they are to be used to communicate with third parties, then they should be subject to the same disclosure regime as other forms of contact. Where exchanges by means of NCCCs are in place of a face-to-face meeting or prompt significant consideration in government, they warrant inclusion in the government transparency releases. If an appropriate transparency regime cannot be found that can command public

confidence, which we consider the current arrangements do not, the use of any NCCCs should be blocked on official devices.[20]

However convenient such devices are, they have created various constitutional dilemmas relating to matters such as accountability, which are core to democracy and more important than being able to use any given communications technology.

Restrictions on political protest

The Conservative government that lost office in 2024 had created and deployed powers that restrict the potential for protest. It justified them on the grounds that they are in response to new techniques and unacceptable degrees of disruption from certain groups. However, the new approach to policing protest has been subject to criticism from numerous observers. For instance, commenting on the Public Order Act 2023, the United National Human Rights Commissioner, Volker Türk, stated in April 2023 that:

This new law imposes serious and undue restrictions on ... rights that are neither necessary nor proportionate to achieve a legitimate purpose as defined under international law. This law is wholly unnecessary as UK police already have the powers to act against violent and disruptive demonstrations ...

It is especially worrying that the law expands the

powers of the police to stop and search individuals, including without suspicion; defines some of the new criminal offences in a vague and overly broad manner; and imposes unnecessary and disproportionate criminal sanctions on people organizing or taking part in peaceful protests.[21]

The demeaning of public institutions by senior politicians

Attacks on institutions such as the BBC, judiciary, and Civil Service by senior politicians, including government ministers, had become common by the early 2020s. In criticism that took on a populist tone, various holders of public office were cast as resisting the will of the people. For instance, when serving as attorney general, Suella Braverman, in a media interview given in July 2022, questioned the professional integrity of civil servants. She was reported as stating that 'some of the biggest battles you face as a minister are, in the nicest possible way, with Whitehall and internally with civil servants, as opposed to your political battles in the chamber'. She complained: 'What I have seen time and time again, both in policymaking and in broader decision making, [is] that there is a Remain bias. I'll say it. I have seen resistance to some of the measures that ministers have wanted to bring forward'.[22]

A related rise of conspiracy theories promoted by mainstream politicians

Connected to this tendency – often in relation to a mythical 'deep state' that works in favour of an alleged 'elite' and to the detriment of elected politicians and 'the people' – two successive prime ministers, Boris Johnson and Liz Truss, both of whom were ousted by their own parliamentary party, have referred to the machinations of a 'deep state' working against them. Johnson did so in the House of Commons on 18 July 2022, while still serving as prime minister, but having in practice conceded his eventual exit from the post. He stated that:

> Some people will say, as I leave office, that this is the end of Brexit ... The Leader of the Opposition and the deep state will prevail in their plot to haul us back into alignment with the EU as a prelude to our eventual return.[23]

The speech Liz Truss made at the Conservative conference during her short premiership, in October 2022, displayed a tendency to see enemies everywhere. Truss referred to a supposed 'anti-growth coalition' consisting of:

> Labour, the Lib Dems and the SNP ... The militant unions, the vested interests dressed up as think-tanks ... The talking heads, the Brexit deniers and Extinction Rebellion ... The fact is they prefer protesting to doing.

They prefer talking on Twitter to taking tough decisions.

They taxi from North London townhouses to the BBC studio to dismiss anyone challenging the status quo.

From broadcast to podcast, they peddle the same old answers.

It's always more taxes, more regulation and more meddling.

Wrong, wrong, wrong ... They don't understand the British people.[24]

On 21 February 2024, Truss told the Conservative Political Action Conference (CPAC) in Maryland, US, that:

I ran for office in 2022 because Britain wasn't growing, the state wasn't delivering, [and] we needed to do more ... I wanted to cut taxes, reduce the administrative state, take back control as people talked about in the Brexit referendum. What I did face was a huge establishment backlash and a lot of it actually came from the state itself ... What has happened in Britain over the past 30 years is power that used to be in the hands of politicians has been moved to quangos and bureaucrats and lawyers so what you find is a democratically elected government actually unable to enact policies ... A quango is a quasi non-governmental organisation. In America you call it the administrative state or the deep state. But we have more than 500 of these quangos in Britain and they run everything ... There's a whole bunch of people – and I describe them as the economic establishment – who fundamentally don't want the status quo to change because they're doing quite fine out of it. They don't really care about the prospects of the average person in Britain and they didn't want things to change and they didn't want that power taken away ... Now people are joining the civil service who are essentially activists ... They might be trans activists, they might be environmental extremists but they are now having a voice within the civil service in a way I don't think was true 30 or 40 years ago. So we just have a wholly new problem and, frankly, a hundred political appointees doesn't even touch the sides in terms of dealing with them.[25]

Truss detected in a wide range of public bodies evidence of a large-scale conspiracy to promote liberal agendas at the expense of the 'average person in Britain' – a populist scenario.

Suspected foreign interference in UK democratic processes

The idea that hostile foreign states might be wielding inappropriate influence on political processes is not new. But it has become particularly salient recently, given the manifest threat posed by powers including

Russia and the creative techniques it has developed in its use of digital communications technology. The part covert Russian activity might have played in the 2016 EU referendum, for instance, has been a subject of extensive interest.[26] The Intelligence and Security Committee of Parliament found in a report published in 2020 (after seemingly being delayed by the government) that:

> There have been widespread public allegations that Russia sought to influence the 2016 referendum on the UK's membership of the EU. The impact of any such attempts would be difficult – if not impossible – to assess, and we have not sought to do so. However, it is important to establish whether a hostile state took deliberate action with the aim of influencing a UK democratic process, irrespective of whether it was successful or not ...

The Committee noted that the Agencies were able to provide it only with scant evidence on this subject, complaining of:

> the extreme caution amongst the intelligence and security Agencies at the thought that they might have any role in relation to the UK's democratic processes, and particularly one as contentious as the EU referendum ... this attitude is illogical; this is about the protection of the process and mechanism from

hostile state interference, which should fall to our intelligence and security Agencies.[27]

Political violence and extremism

Various observers have noted cause for concern about disruptive and even violent threats to democracy from different parts of the political spectrum. For instance, in July 2022, the Intelligence and Security Committee of Parliament published a report into *Extreme Right-Wing Terrorism*.[28] In his 2024 report to the government on political violence and disruption, Lord Walney found that:

> The right to express dissent is a fundamental tenet of our liberal democracy and must be protected. Yet the UK has a growing problem with extreme protest movements that use political violence, intimidation, incitement, law breaking, and disruption. Extreme political activists are targeting core *elements of Britain's democracy*, including elected representatives, the free press, and educational settings ... It is beyond question that we must uphold the right to protest, but so too must we defend our democracy from the tactics of extremists who seek to impose their beliefs on the rest of society with non-democratic and illegal activism.[29]

In the wake of the riots of summer 2024, Home Secretary Yvette Cooper announced a review of the official approach taken to various forms of extremism.[30]

Concerns held by the Public Accounts Committee and other bodies about probity in decision-taking involving large sums of public money

Various revelations about incidents and practices connected to matters such as the awarding of pandemic contracts; the allocation of levelling-up funds; the conferral of peerages; and suspected violations of the *Ministerial Code* have combined to undermine the reputation of the UK with regard to public-sector financial integrity. In January 2023, Transparency International, an anti-corruption campaign group, reported poor performance by the UK in its annual international Corruption Perception Index. In the 2022 Index the UK dropped to its lowest score since the exercise had begun in its current form in 2012, dropping to eighteenth place from eleventh the previous year. In the report, the Chief Executive of Transparency International UK stated that:

> This sharp fall in the UK's score is a powerful indictment of a recent decline in standards in government and controls over the use of taxpayer money ... The underlying data clearly indicate[s] that business executives and other experts are concerned about insufficient controls on the abuse of public office and increasingly view corruption and bribery as a real issue in Britain.[31]

Of the preceding concerns, perhaps the most serious, because of their implications for the underlying integrity of the system, are those involving pressure on the rule of law, the bypassing of fuller law-making procedures through delegated legislation, and possible irregularities in the use of public money. All of these difficulties could be lessened if politicians were more willing to adhere to the 'good chaps' principle, and not insist upon worrying courses of action. These sit alongside the challenges to representative democracy posed by the 2016 referendum. However, as this stress test suggests, pressures on the constitutional and democratic system have a habit of manifesting themselves. They do so in ways that are hard to predict in advance, but can prove highly disruptive. A frequent feature of them is that they involve people in positions of authority manipulating the system or departing from established norms. We cannot exclude more drastic misbehaviour of this type taking place in future.

Conclusion

The well-being, viability, and vitality of our parliamentary democracy represents the first line of defence of the realm. Over the bulk of our lifetimes most of our fellow countrymen and women – if they think about it at all – take an almost perverse pleasure in the impenetrable elusiveness of our constitution, which fits neatly with our appetite for muddling through. Commit it all to paper and the bloom would be gone. However, ours is not a time for claims that 'it'll be alright on the night' or any other soothing lullabies of national complacency; nor the belief in 'muddling through' as the primary principle of our way of governing ourselves.

Recent experience, along with possible future trajectories, suggest both that there are weaknesses in our system and people ready to exploit them; and ideas that might drive them to do so. We need to take these threats seriously, and act accordingly.

If we fail to take a long, hard look at the state of our defences against potential authoritarianism, creeping or sudden, it would not be merely a matter of the 'good chaps' theory of government finding a final resting place in the British Museum and a gradual further deterioration in the quality and civility of our national political conversation; the centuries' work that has gone into the making of our open democratic society could be undone in the space of a few years or, in the case of the 'limpet prime minister' scenario, a few days. And the culpability would be ours. For we ourselves will have thrown it away through a combination of insouciance and inadvertence on the part of the many, and malign intent on the part of a few.

It *could* happen here.

Notes

Part One: The Limpet Prime Minister

1 The phrase is Lord Lisvane's. Conversation with Peter Hennessy.

2 'King Charles III's address to the nation and Commonwealth in full', *BBC News* (9 September 2022), accessed online.

3 'His Majesty The King's Declaration', royal.uk, accessed online.

4 'His Majesty The King's reply to addresses of condolence at Westminster Hall', royal.uk, accessed online.

5 Laura Kuenssberg, 'Labour must deliver or risk populist rise – ministers', *BBC News* (22 July 2024), accessed online.

6 Hannah Shrimpton and Gideon Skinner, '85 per cent say Britain is divided as concern about extremism rises', Ipsos (22 August 2024), accessed online.

7 'Director General Ken McCallum gives latest threat update', MI5 (8 October 2024), accessed online.

8   Hansard, 'Safety of Rwanda (Asylum and
    Immigration) Bill', HL Deb. (29 January 2024), vol.
    835, col. 1022, accessed online.
9   John Henley, 'Younger people more likely to doubt
    merits of democracy – global poll', *Guardian* (11
    September 2023), accessed online.
10 Roy Jenkins, 'Past and Future', in Anthony Lester
    (ed.), *Essays and Speeches* (London, 1967), 136–9,
    136.
11 Ernest Gellner, *Plough, Sword and Book: The
    Structure of Human History* (Chicago, 1988), 274.

Part Two: Protecting the System

1   See, for example: Clive Walker, *Blackstone's Guide to
    The Anti-Terrorism Legislation* (Oxford, 2014).
2   See, for example: A. W. Brian Simpson, *In the
    Highest Degree Odious: Detention without Trial in
    Wartime Britain* (Oxford, 1992).
3   Peter Hennessy, *The Secret State: Whitehall and the
    Cold War* (London, 2002), 154–5.
4   For an investigation of political violence, conducted
    for the Conservative government, see: Lord Walney,
    Protecting Our Democracy from Coercion, HC 775
    (21 May 2024), accessed online.
5   William Waldegrave, *The Binding of Leviathan:
    Conservatism and the Future* (London, 1978), 74.
6   See, for example: Dennis Barker, 'Obituary:
    General Sir Walter Walker', *Guardian* (14 August
    2001), accessed online.

7   HM Government, *Ministerial Code* (London, 2024) and *The Cabinet Manual: A guide to the laws, conventions and rules on the operation of government*, first edition (London, 2011), both accessed online.

8   Bagehot goes on to state that 'a king of great sense and sagacity would want no others'. Walter Bagehot, *The English Constitution*, (Oxford, 2001; first edition 1867), 64. Bagehot has formed part of the core reading list on the syllabus of constitutional tutelage for successive monarchs since George V.

9   'The Speaker of the House of Commons', *Erskine May: Parliamentary Practice* (London, 2019), paragraph 4.19.

10 David Torrance, *The office and role of Speaker* (London, 2024), 8, accessed online.

11 For a recent overview of these powers and their status, see: Robert Hazell and Timothy Foot, *Executive Power: The Prerogative, Past, Present, and Future* (London, 2022).

12 See, for example: Jack Simson Caird, *Impeachment* (London, 2016), accessed online.

13 Peter Hennessy, *The Secret State: Preparing for the Worst 1945–2010* (London, 2010), 356–7.

14 The phrase is Philip Ziegler's. Conversation with PH, 13 June 1991.

15 See the 2022–3 Financial Statements: 'Security and Intelligence Agencies Financial Statements 2022–23 (HTML)', HC 1797 (22 September 2023), accessed online.

16 Our metaphor of 'the lining nerve of the self: consciousness' is drawn from Michael Frayn's *The Human Touch: Our Part in the Creation of a Universe* (London, 2006), 399.

17 Blick and Hennessy, *Bonfire of the Decencies*, 131–3.

Part Three: The Ten-Year Stress Test

1 Oscar Wilde, *The Importance of Being Earnest*, Act III.

2 Committee on Standards in Public Life, *The Seven Principles of Public Life*, gov.uk (31 May 1995), accessed online.

3 Blick and Hennessy, *Bonfire of the Decencies*, 17–21.

4 House of Commons Committee of Privileges, *Matter referred on 21 April 2022 (conduct of Rt Hon Boris Johnson): Final Report*, HC 564 (London, 2023), 7, accessed online.

5 House of Commons Committee of Privileges, *Matter referred on 21 April 2022: Co-ordinated campaign of interference in the work of the Privileges Committee*, HC 1652 (London, 2023), 3, accessed online.

6 Blick and Hennessy, *Bonfire of the Decencies,* 17–21.

7 'Cabinet was not informed of plans to scrap top rate of tax, Truss says', *Reuters* (2 October 2022), accessed online.

8 Jill Rutter, 'Suella Braverman's collective responsibility problem was just one reason for

Sunak to sack her', *Institute for Government* (11 November 2023), accessed online.

9   'R (on the application of Miller) (Appellant) v. The Prime Minister (Respondent)' and 'Cherry and others (Respondents) v. Advocate General for Scotland (Appellant) (Scotland)', [2019] UKSC 41 (Judgment date 24 September 2019), 20–2, accessed online.

10 '"A dangerous precedent": Raab's letter of resignation and Sunak's reply in full', *Guardian* (21 April 2023), accessed online.

11 'Resignation statement in full as Boris Johnson steps down', *BBC News* (8 June 2023), accessed online.

12 Civil Service, *Civil Service code*, gov.uk (updated 15 March 2015), accessed online.

13 House of Lords Select Committee on the Constitution, *Permanent Secretaries: their appointment and removal*, HL Paper 258 (London, 2023), 7, accessed online.

14 Civil Service, *Civil Service code*.

15 '"A dangerous precedent"', *Guardian*.

16 Lizzie Dearden, 'Suella Braverman say it is her "dream" and "obsession" to see a flight take asylum seekers to Rwanda', *Independent* (5 October 2022), accessed online.

17 Hansard Society, *Delegated Legislation Review* (London, 2021), accessed online.

18 House of Lords Secondary Legislation Scrutiny Committee, *Government by Diktat: A call to return power to Parliament*, HL Paper 105 (London, 2021), 2, accessed online.

19 House of Lords Delegated Powers and Regulatory Reform Committee, *Democracy Denied? The urgent need to rebalance power between Parliament and the Executive*, HL Paper 106 (London, 2021), 3–4, accessed online.

20 House of Commons Public Administration and Constitutional Affairs Committee, *Lobbying and Influence: post-legislative scrutiny of the Lobbying Act 2014 and related matters*, HC 203 (London, 2024), 14–15, accessed online.

21 United Nations Office of the Human Rights Commissioner, 'UN Human Rights Chief urges UK to reverse "deeply troubling" Public Order Bill' (27 April 2023), accessed online.

22 Beckie Smith, 'Attorney General's "Remain bias" jibe "damaging to civil service morale"', *Civil Service World* (4 July 2022), accessed online.

23 Hansard, 'Confidence in Her Majesty's Government', HC Deb. (18 July 2022), vol. 718, col. 732, accessed online.

24 Sophie Wingate, 'Liz Truss rails against "anti-growth coalition" including speech hecklers', *Independent* (5 October 2022), accessed online.

25 David Smith, 'Britain's "deep state" thwarted my plans, Liz Truss tells US far-right summit', *Guardian* (22 February 2024), accessed online.

26 See, for example: House of Commons Digital, Culture, Media and Sport Committee, *Disinformation and 'fake news': Final Report*, HC 1791 (London, 2019), 70, accessed online.

27 Intelligence and Security Committee of Parliament, *Russia*, HC 632 (London, 21 July 2020), 12–13, accessed online.

28 Intelligence and Security Committee of Parliament, *Extreme Right-Wing Terrorism* (London, 13 July 2022), accessed online.

29 Lord Walney, *Protecting Our Democracy from Coercion*, HC 775 (May 2024), 8, accessed online. Emphasis added.

30 Helen Catt and Charlotte Rose, 'Misogyny to be treated as extremism by UK government', *BBC News* (18 August 2024), accessed online.

31 'UK plunges to lowest ever position in Corruption Perceptions Index', *Transparency International UK* (31 January 2023), accessed online.